HOW TO HANDLE DIFFICULT PEOPLE

Vernon Howard

© 1996 New Life Foundation
Pine, AZ 85544
Reprinted 2000

ISBN 0-911203-28-1

LET THIS BOOKLET
WORK FOR YOU

Would you like to reply to a foolish world with power and poise? You can.

Select any section you like. Thoughtfully read the seven answers. ***Remember, you do not actually speak the answers aloud to another person.*** The answers are designed to build right and strong attitudes within you. And, of course they are not said as angry accusations; you are merely seeing obvious facts about the person. These *silent* answers will build your firmness and understanding. You will learn how to avoid the traps of cunning people.

These answers are really very kindly, for they come from a high source of strength and wisdom. It is weakness and confusion toward people that is unkind, for it keeps them undeveloped. So have no guilt in seeing thru deceitful men and women. You have a right to free spiritual speech, and it returns a rich inner reward. When you truly understand a harmful person you are free of him, so let these answers dissolve all problems with people.

The world has a desperate need for strong people who know and live the real answers to life. Be one of them.

Vernon Howard

WHEN PEOPLE INTERFERE
WITH YOUR LIFE

1. Please do not use my personal affairs for your private entertainment.

2. What do you secretly expect in return for your help?

3. You pretend to help because you know of nothing else to do with yourself.

4. The greatest help you can give me is to leave me alone.

5. If I wish your help I will ask for it.

6. How would you feel if I asked *you* a personal question like that?

7. Your kind of help just adds to the problem.

TO SEE HIDDEN MOTIVES IN PEOPLE

8. If I exposed your actual motives, what would they be?

9. I predict that you will depart once you see that you cannot use me.

10. If you only knew how clearly I see thru you.

11. One of your pretenses is the pretense that you don't want anything from me.

12. Is your outer niceness matched by inner pleasantness?

13. I wonder what you are trying to hide from me.

14. From now on I will see you as you really are, not as I want to see you.

WHEN PEOPLE UNLOAD
THEIR TROUBLES ONTO YOU

15. The person who caused his own problem is the only one who can solve it.

16. I will not injure you by doing your work.

17. You don't want solutions—you just want to talk about yourself.

18. No, I do not accept *your* difficulties as being *my* difficulties.

19. It is wrong to help someone when it prevents him from learning the lesson.

20. You alone are responsible for your own life.

21. You are wasting your time urging me to feel sorry for you.

HOW MEN CAN REPLY
TO WOMEN

22. Your tears are more cunning than influential.

23. I was not placed here on earth just to please you.

24. If you want to be sour then I want to be absent.

25. I have no interest in making your burdens my burdens.

26. By declining your favors I avoid your traps.

27. You are a skilled actress but I see thru the performance.

28. I want a pleasant relationship, not a contest between two egos.

HOW WOMEN CAN
REPLY TO MEN

29. I wish your spirit was as strong as your sex drive.

30. How long will you use me before leaving?

31. For the first time I suspect that you are not really good for me.

32. My mind is not at the mercy of your mind.

33. I need understanding of life more than I need you.

34. My insight into you frees me from your falseness.

35. My *no* to you is final.

TO A CRUEL
HUMAN BEING

36. If you wish to torment yourself with your own cruelty, that is up to you.

37. Can't you see that viciousness is living its life thru you?

38. What a sick pleasure you take in hurting others.

39. As long as you refuse to admit your brutality you will remain its victim.

40. Unfortunately, you can't see that your cruelty is also your stupidity.

41. Honestly, now, how do you like living with yourself?

42. Your one chance is to see that cruelty's excitement is not the same as true life.

TO SLANDERERS OF
TRUTH AND DECENCY

43. After watching you I now know the meaning of self-destructive behavior.

44. True goodness cannot come from a hard and hostile person.

45. Your method is very simple—you sneer at truths you are incapable of understanding.

46. You are nervous because you are lost.

47. Since rightness has no need to prove itself, I wonder why you argue so much.

48. I suggest that you take a dictionary and look up the word *blasphemy*.

49. Your agony is that you travel full speed to your destination—but you don't know what it is.

WHEN PEOPLE TRY TO MAKE YOU FEEL GUILTY

50. This is just another trick of yours to evade your own responsibilities.

51. There is no way you can make *me* feel guilty over *your* mistakes.

52. For spiritual growth I must explain myself to myself, but I owe you no explanation.

53. I am not required to sacrifice my life to you.

54. When you avoid your own guilt you also avoid your chance for self-healing.

55. You call it standing up for your rights, but I call it infantile bad manners.

56. How strange that *I* always owe *you* something, but never the reverse.

TO A DEPRESSED AND DEFEATED PERSON

57. I sense a lot of violence in your gloom.

58. You should try to see what a harmful influence you are on yourself.

59. What if everyone on earth went around like you?

60. Unfortunately, you accept defeat as normal and necessary.

61. I am very alert to not fall under the influence of your dishonest spirit.

62. Your self-pity is both unkind and unspiritual.

63. My life is devoted to my enlightenment, not to your self-chosen darkness.

FOR PROTECTION FROM EVIL PEOPLE

64. One fact is clear in my mind—I don't really need you.

65. You don't know it, but I remain at a safe inner distance from you.

66. Too bad you can't take truth as easily as you give falsehood.

67. There is no way you can disturb me unless I carelessly permit it.

68. Is nothing too low for you to do?

69. It is all very simple—your badness can never be good for me.

70. Your problem is that you just won't face that you just don't know.

TO ARROGANT PEOPLE WITH TEMPORARY POWER

71. You are nothing more than a prominent and foolish human being.

72. There is such a thing as a psychological criminal, and you are one of them.

73. What will happen to you when you finally lose your authority?

74. Your life is meaningless and both of us know it.

75. You think you are normal, which is just what keeps you abnormal.

76. What you call leadership is simply your attempt to escape your own emptiness.

77. Wake up and see what you are doing *against yourself.*

FOR HELPFUL INSIGHTS
INTO PEOPLE

78. You take delusion as reality and take correction as attack.

79. I notice that when you tell me what is right it is always right for *you*.

80. You think your judgment is your understanding, which it is not.

81. Natural behavior is an utter stranger to you.

82. You insist you are right, yet you are the most insecure person I know.

83. What a strange way you have of relieving pressure—you just blame someone else.

84. You *love* to hate and be hated, for it keeps attention on yourself.

TO SOMEONE WITH SELF-DEFEATING ATTITUDES

85. The one way you can be right is to admit you are wrong.

86. Your problem is your refusal to see anything higher than yourself.

87. The only thing you have to be is real.

88. Now that you have won your demand, how will it make you happy?

89. Truth alone will never betray and hurt you.

90. Stop asking falsehood for directions.

91. You suffer from a bad dream, which will vanish with inner awakening.

WHEN WITH
AN ANGRY PERSON

92. Your anger has no authority to tell me to tremble.

93. I see your rage as being childish, not forceful.

94. If you want a destructive fight you will have to fight all alone.

95. I see the false thrill you get from your outburst, and also see the dreadful price you pay.

96. You have just shown me a perfect example of exploding egotism.

97. Is foolish fury the only response of which you are capable?

98. Sorry, but I no longer believe in the power of your anger.

TO DEMANDING AND INTIMIDATING TYRANTS

99. My life belongs to *me*, not to your cruel threats.

100. I wish to be who I am, not who you demand I should be.

101. Your angry accusation is caused by your insecurity, not by my refusal to you.

102. What law says I must behave according to your demands?

103. I am not an actor who must obey your script.

104. Your intimidation is weakness, not strength.

105. I remain safe, for my understanding of you is stronger than your screams.

TO PEOPLE WHO DRAIN YOUR ENERGY

106. What I used to call our friendship I now see as a mutual draining of energy.

107. I need my own time to develop my own inner life.

108. Human activities consist of little children playing games and exchanging toys.

109. I just can't afford you anymore.

110. It took me awhile, but I finally saw that I was socializing my life away.

111. My aim is to live from *myself*, not from relatives and friends.

112. I want what truth has to give, not what society falsely promises.

TO PEOPLE WHO NEED SHOCKING FACTS

113. Each time you trick another person you trick yourself.

114. You cherish your violent thoughts and then claim that you want peace of mind.

115. What hypocrisy to think of yourself as an innocent victim.

116. Nothing blocks your happiness but your own preference for self-ignorance.

117. To demand self-glory is to invite self-disaster.

118. Can't you see that merely calling yourself wise does not banish stupidity?

119. For a whole year you should study the meaning of *unconscious egotism.*

FOR RIGHT STERNNESS
WITH PEOPLE

120. Love consists of not agreeing with your hatred.

121. I refuse to excuse your ignorant behavior.

122. Your hostility proves that you are unteachable, which relieves me of helping you.

123. I will not join or defend your harmful position.

124. Your fondness for flattering lies is ruining your life.

125. You have absolutely nothing of true value to give me.

126. I wish to follow my own real nature, which means I cannot follow you.

TO PEOPLE WHO NEED REFRESHING TRUTH

127. Realize that defense of your wrong position is defeat for your life.

128. If you can't take it you won't make it.

129. It is not necessary for you to pretend that all is well.

130. Learn to listen, and reality will show you how to drop false duties.

131. Lose your wrong beliefs and you will lose your problems.

132. No longer value your complaints, for they are worthless.

133. See what life is *really* all about, not what you *assume* it is all about.

TO SELF-RIGHTEOUS HYPOCRITES

134. You talk about love, but why do I see hatred in your words?

135. I see clearly what you really are— a smiling hypocrite.

136. Who said that your morals are superior to mine?

137. You promise me a future heaven but you want yours in the here and now.

138. Are you an example of what you teach?

139. You should be ashamed of yourself, but you may be too far gone for shame.

140. If you are a pilot thru life, I am getting off the airplane.

TO WEAK AND
DEPENDENT PEOPLE

141. I don't agree that your lack of self-responsibility is my problem.

142. You suffer from a refusal to learn.

143. I am not required to sacrifice my life to your weakness.

144. It is against spiritual law to help you when you won't help yourself.

145. I have not hired out to be your servant.

146. You wrongly take self-reliance as a burden, when it is really a natural pleasure.

147. Your weakness is simply a wrong choice which you can change whenever you like.

TO A RUDE AND INSOLENT PERSON

148. Your aim is to cause distress in me—and you will fail.

149. I refuse to descend to your level of insolence.

150. You have helped me to see that I must never become like you.

151. How odd that you rudely blast others but demand courtesy in return.

152. You have shown me that rudeness has no problem finding a target.

153. If you could only see that you do not know what you think you know.

154. You criticize my plan, so what is your superior plan?

TO PEOPLE WHO CAN'T STOP TALKING

155. Your words don't even make sense to you, which you fear to see.

156. You can't even see your non-stop talking as the bad manners that it is.

157. Does it occur to you that I don't want to hear what you want to say?

158. You call your talkativeness a helpful contribution, when it is really a compulsive conceit.

159. What a dreadful waste of energy that could be used for self-awakening.

160. You talk yourself right out of a free and happy life.

161. A million words can't uplift your spirit one inch, but you still talk on.

WHEN PEOPLE TRY TO DECEIVE YOU

162. You have the wrong man.

163. What you really want is for mine to become yours.

164. Believe me, I know a hoax when I see one, and I see one.

165. Why do you find it necessary to keep telling me how sincere you are?

166. I decline to agree with the virtues you credit to yourself.

167. You might have fooled me when I was eighteen.

168. You just gave yourself away with a flash of anger you failed to hide.

FOR FREEDOM FROM
FALSE HELPERS

169. You know everything except how to handle your own life.

170. I wish a solid branch, not a shaky twig.

171. You want to save me but I really need to be saved from you.

172. It is clear that you want me to change my mind for your own benefit.

173. You are hurting yourself trying to make your wrong look like right.

174. My wish is to have healing, not your false comfort.

175. Your kind of help has kept the world in chains.

TO BAD AND SCHEMING PEOPLE

176. You flatter me only to control me.

177. Regardless of what you choose, I choose inner light.

178. I decline to join your folly, and that is that.

179. My involvements with you prove the value of solitude.

180. I don't know what you want, but I want my life to make sense.

181. It is clear that you plan to use me and abandon me.

182. I wish to know what I really want in life, not what you say I want.

TO CONFUSED AND NERVOUS PEOPLE

183. Something can be done *for* you when something can be done *with* you.

184. To make your life better, start with self-honesty.

185. I see in your face your years of breaking the laws of higher life.

186. The only question is, do you want to learn or do you want to argue?

187. You think the truth is harsh, when it is really that you are harsh.

188. Try to see that your confusion is a sign of something wrong with your inner self.

189. If you want to *feel* right you need only *be* right.

TO PEOPLE WHO NEED ACCURATE ADVICE

190. Truth will show you how to stop those painful mental movies.

191. Your kind of rightness is wrecking your life.

192. You can feel persecuted or you can feel happy, but you can't feel both.

193. Since you suffer from yourself, where must the cure start?

194. You change your disguises so often you don't know who you are.

195. Have no fear whatever of dropping your habitual nature.

196. As a helpful experiment, send out an invitation to higher ideas to visit you.

WHEN DOMINEERING PEOPLE FRIGHTEN YOU

197. Your demand for power exposes you as a very insecure human being.

198. I will not feed your neurosis by fearing you.

199. How amazing that you are always right and I am always wrong.

200. I do not give my consent to your domination of me.

201. My fear of you is simply a wrong reaction which truth will correct.

202. I simply see you as a very hostile person with a serious problem to solve.

203. You are harsh and unkind simply because you do not know any other way to behave.

TO SOMEONE WHO FIGHTS
SPIRITUAL TEACHINGS

204. How strange that you cannot see that you are your own danger.

205. It is your egotism that takes spiritual facts as being insulting.

206. Why do you cling to what is injuring you?

207. Your self-deception is your prison which you refuse to see.

208. Realize that your painful world is not the only world that exists.

209. If you know the answers to life, how come you are so nervous?

210. Sometime just try to listen to something higher than your neurosis.

TO A CHILDISH PERSON

211. When you bring your complaining self-pity to me, you have come to the wrong place.

212. My advice to you is to grow up.

213. Please see that you have to live with and suffer from your own immaturity.

214. Do you seek the answers you need or the answers you demand?

215. After getting hurt by carelessly walking into a wall you blame the wall.

216. Try to see that *you* cause *your* problems.

217. You would be shocked to learn what people really think of you.

FOR REAL INDEPENDENCE FROM PEOPLE

218. Since freedom can never be wrong, I end all false ties to you.

219. Neither your approval nor your disapproval tell me how to feel.

220. I allowed you to think for me, and now see what it cost.

221. We will have either a pleasant relationship or none at all.

222. I will no longer be loyal to anyone who is hurting my life.

223. My life belongs to me, not to you.

224. I will not take your word for anything—I want to know what is right *from myself*.

Please show this booklet to a friend, counselor or church leader. He or she will appreciate seeing these dynamic and healthy truths.

NEW LIFE FOUNDATION
PO Box 2230
Pine, Arizona 85544
(520) 476-3224
E-mail: info@anewlife.org
www.anewlife.org

New Area Code • 928

ABOUT VERNON HOWARD

Vernon Howard broke through to another world. He saw through the illusion of suffering and fear and loneliness. From 1965 until his death in 1992 he wrote books and conducted classes which reflect a degree of skill and understanding that may be unsurpassed in modern history. Tape recordings of many of his class talks are available.

Today more than 8 million readers worldwide enjoy his exceptionally clear and inspiring presentations of the great truths of the ages. His books are widely used by doctors, psychiatrists, psychologists, counselors, clergymen, educators and people from all walks of life. All his teachings center around the one grand theme: *There is a way out of the human problem and anyone can find it.*

"People find it hard to believe that Truth exists on earth for those who really want it. Truth seems so out of place in this desperate world, like a book of poems on a battlefield. People cannot see Truth because of misplaced attention. They attend to the social battle because they wrongly think they must be winners. But the battle really exists only in their misused minds, which Truth wants them to see. The seeing is the healing."

"Think beyond yourself. Feel beyond yourself. Walk beyond yourself. Why? Because this is what a certain part of you wants more than anything else. Make it the supreme part."

—Vernon Howard

700 Inspiring Guides to a New Life
(See special offer on next page)

(See special offer on next page)

ORDER FORM

☐ **SPECIAL INTRODUCTORY OFFER**

Receive the following Vernon Howard
book, cassette tape and booklet—*Only $12*

- *700 Inspiring Guides to a New Life* · Book-192 pp
- *Secrets the Whole World Should Hear* · Cassette
- *Conquer Anxiety and Frustration* · Booklet-40 pp

ALL FOR ONLY $12! • *SAVE $8*
(includes shipping)

☐ Please send me free literature.

My check or money order for $_____
is enclosed.

Name _____

Address _____ Apt _____

City _____

State _____ Zip _____

Send to: **NEW LIFE • PO Box 2230
Pine, Arizona 85544**

XSDIF

NOTES